Food from the World

Alan Trussell-Cullen

First published in 2007 by Cengage Learning Australia
www.cengage.com.au

This edition published in 2008 under the imprint of Nelson Thornes Ltd,
Delta Place, 27 Bath Road, Cheltenham, United Kingdom, GL53 7TH

10 9 8 7 6 5 4 3 2
11 10 09 08

Text © 2007 Alan Trussell-Cullen

The right of Alan Trussell-Cullen to be identified as author of this work has been asserted by him/her in accordance with the Copyright, Designs and Patents Act 1988

All rights reserved. No part of this publication may be reproduced or transmitted in any form or by any means, electronic or mechanical, including photocopy, recording or any information storage and retrieval system, without permission in writing from the publisher or under licence from the Copyright Licensing Agency Limited, of 90 Tottenham Court Road, London W1T 4LP.

Any person who commits any unauthorised act in relation to this publication may be
liable to criminal prosecution and civil claims for damages.

Food from the World
ISBN 978-1-4085-0055-2

Text by Alan Trussell-Cullen
Illustrations by Vonda Pestana
Edited by Kate McGough
Series Design by James Lowe
Designed by Vonda Pestana
Production Controller Hanako Smith
Audio recordings by Juliet Hill, Picture Start
Spoken by Matthew King and Abbe Holmes
Printed in China by 1010 Printing International Ltd

Website www.nelsonthornes.com

Acknowledgements
The author and publisher would like to acknowledge permission to reproduce material from
the following sources:
Photographs by Australian Picture Library/ Corbis/ George D. Lepp, p. 13 left; Getty Images/ Stone, front cover, p. 1; Liquid Library, pp. 3 top, 5 bottom right; Newspix/ Graham Crouch, p. 7; Photodisc, p. 10; Photolibrary.com/ Ifa-Bilderteam Gmbh, p. 9/ Jon Arnold Images, p. 8/ Rosenfeld, pp. 5 centre top, 5 top right, 13 right/ Selly Laszlo, p. 5 bottom left/ Southern Stock, p. 11/ Edith Laue, p. 12 bottom/ AGE Fotostock/ Kevin O'Hara, p. 12 top; Photos.com, back cover, pp. 3 bottom, 4, 5 top left, 5 centre left, 6, 16.

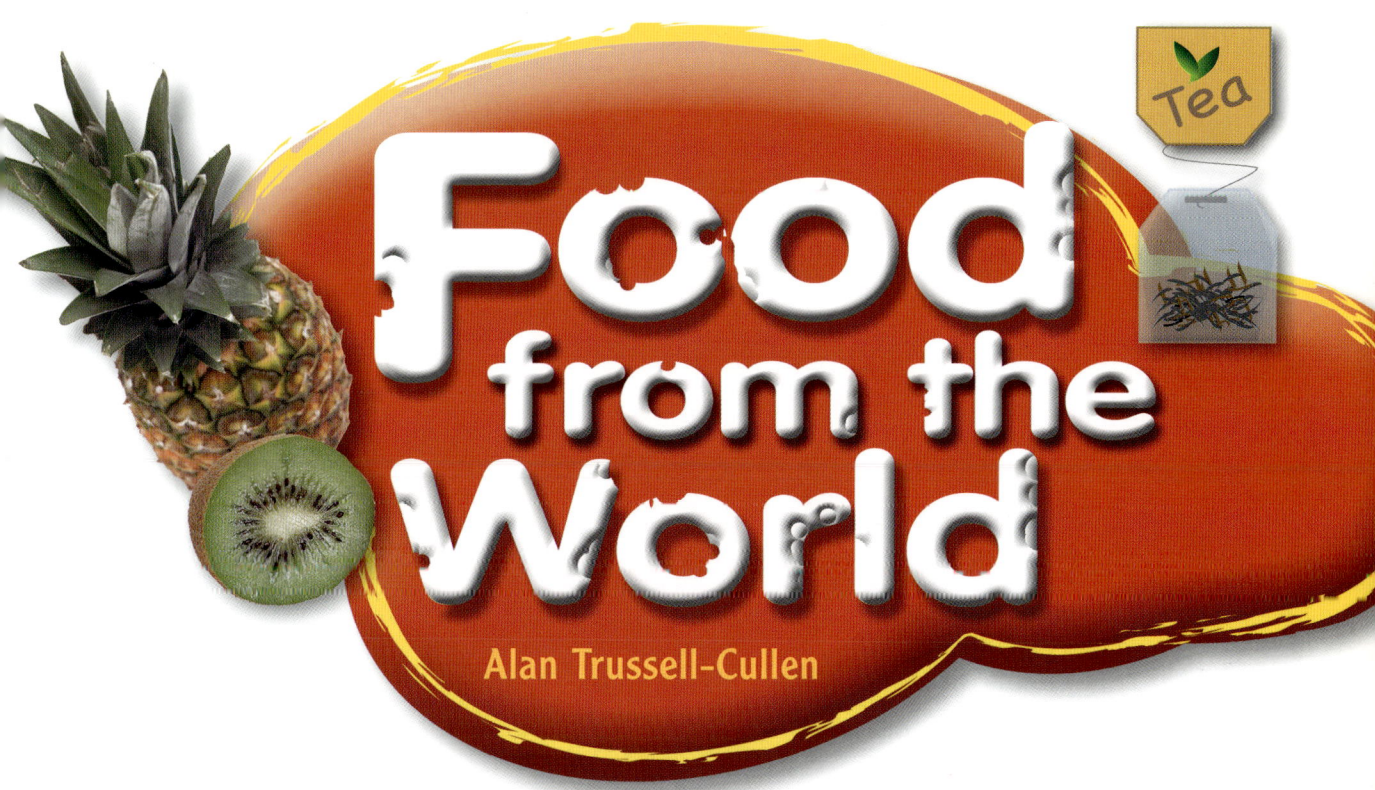

Food from the World

Alan Trussell-Cullen

Contents

Chapter 1	Food from the World	4
Chapter 2	Bananas	6
Chapter 3	Rice and Tea	8
Chapter 4	Pineapples and Kiwi Fruit	10
Chapter 5	Dates and Raisins	12
Chapter 6	Where in the World?	14
Index		16

Chapter 1

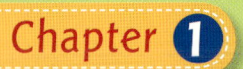

Food from the World

Look at all this food.

Some of the food comes from nearby.

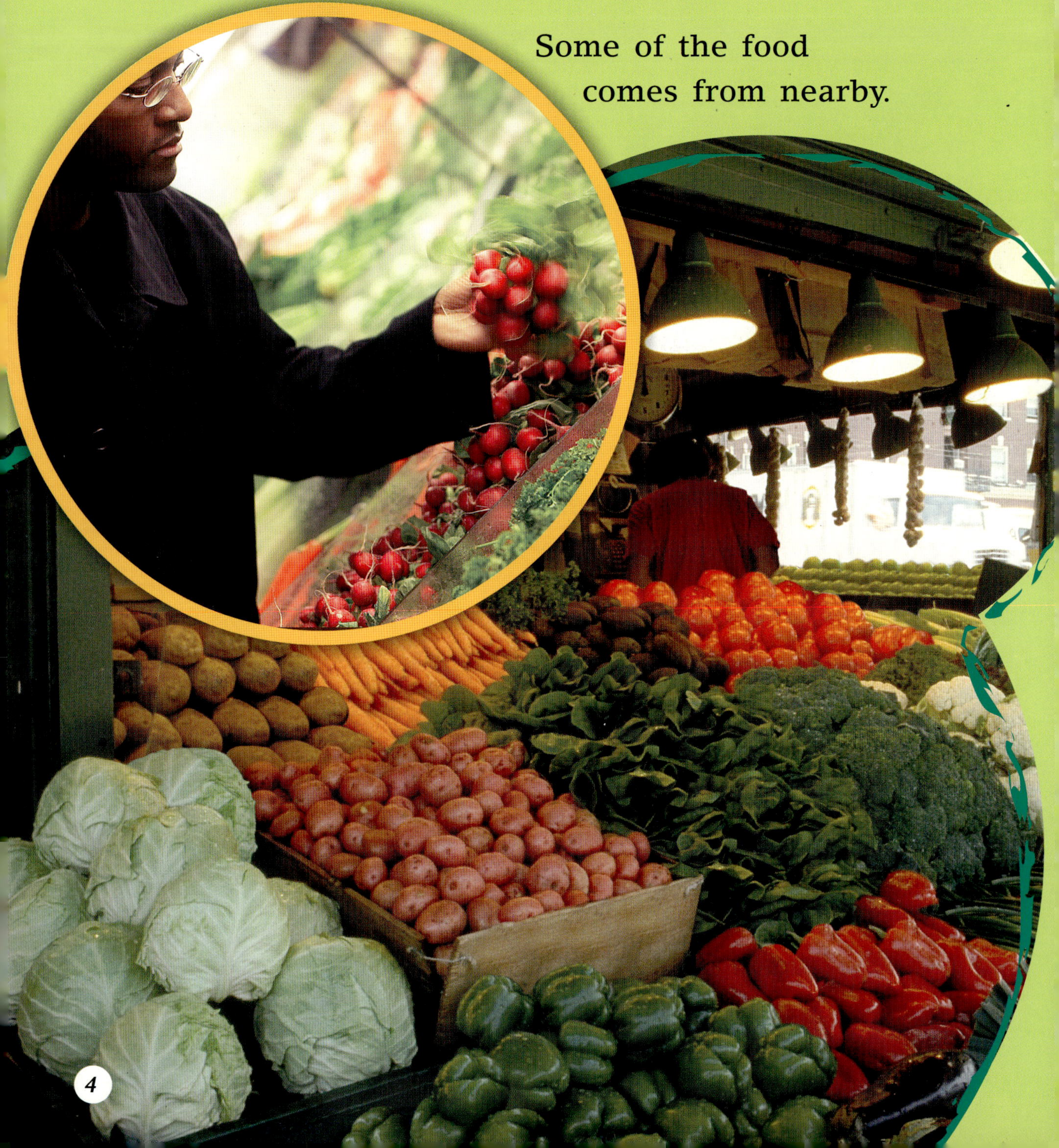

But a lot of it comes from countries all over the world.

Here are some of the foods we eat in Europe.

- kiwi fruit
- bananas
- dates
- raisins
- rice
- tea
- pineapple

Chapter 2

Bananas

Bananas grow in South America, Australia and Africa.

Bananas grow on banana palm trees. They need a lot of sun.

When the bananas are green, it is time to take them off the tree.

Bananas grow here.
South America
Africa
Australia

Chapter 3

Rice and Tea

Rice grows all over the world. A lot of rice comes from China, Australia and the USA.

Rice grows well where it is wet.

Tea grows in a lot of countries.
A lot of tea comes from India and China.
Tea can be black or green.

Chapter 4

Pineapples and Kiwi Fruit

Pineapples grow in countries that have lots of sun.
A lot of pineapples come from Australia, South America and the USA.

Kiwi fruit are brown.
They can be green or yellow
on the inside.

A lot of kiwi fruit comes from New Zealand.
Kiwi fruit came to New Zealand
from China.
A lot of kiwi fruit comes from
South America and the USA, too.

Chapter 5
Dates and Raisins

Dates grow in Africa.
They need a lot of sun.
Dates grow on date palm trees.

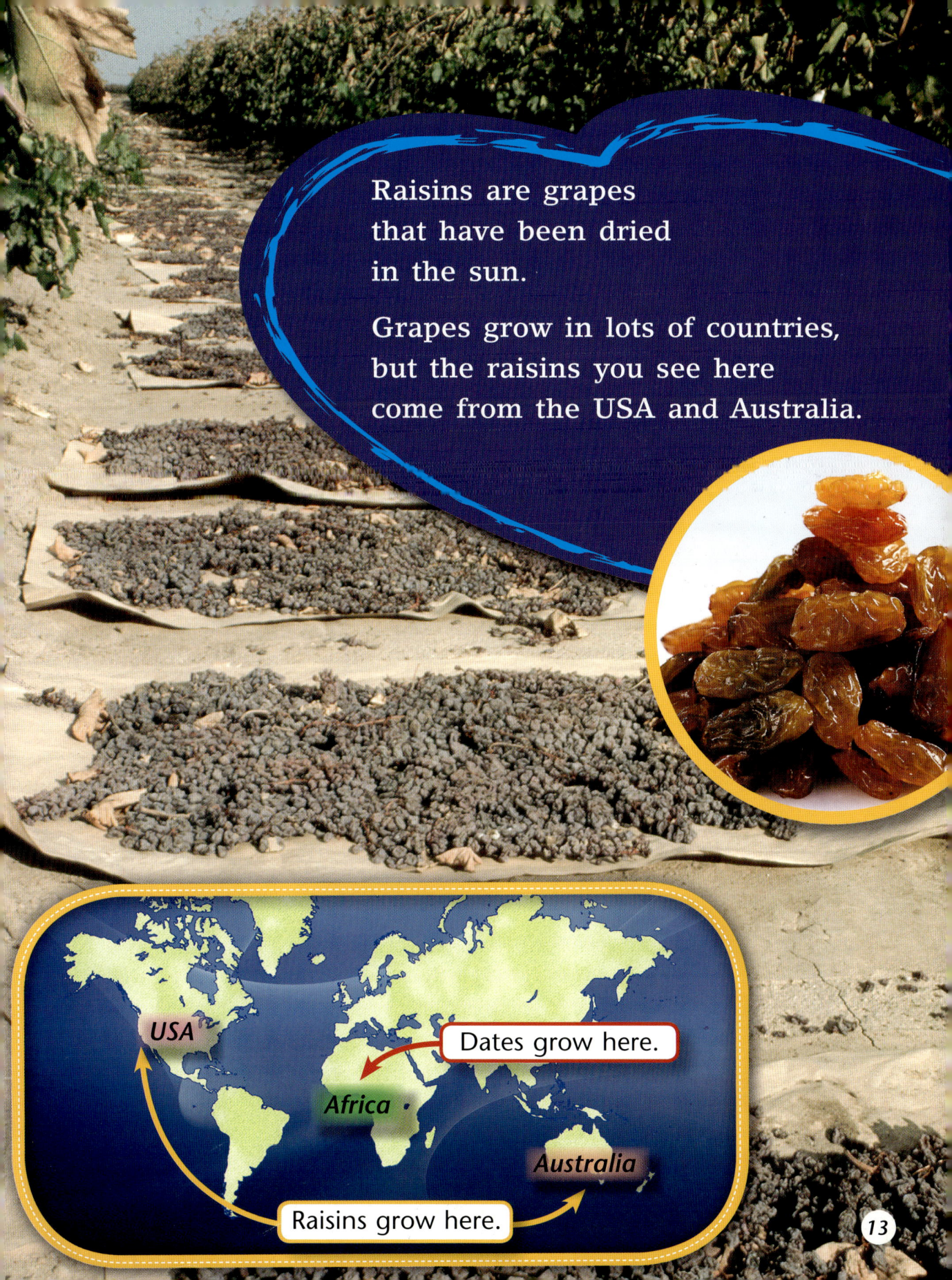

Raisins are grapes that have been dried in the sun.

Grapes grow in lots of countries, but the raisins you see here come from the USA and Australia.

USA

Dates grow here.

Africa

Australia

Raisins grow here.

Chapter 6

Where in the World?

- bananas
- rice
- tea
- pineapples
- kiwi fruit
- dates
- raisins

Europe

USA

South America

Food grows all over the world. Today the food we eat can come from a country a long way from home.

Index

bananas   5, 6–7, 14–15

dates   5, 12, 13, 14–15

kiwi fruit   5, 10, 11, 14–15

pineapples   5, 10, 14–15

raisins   5, 13, 14–15

rice   5, 8, 9, 14–15

tea   5, 9, 14–15